KALEIDOSCOPE

THE PONY EXPRESS

by
Edward F. Dolan

Benchmark Books

MARSHALL CAVENDISH
NEW YORK

Benchmark Books
Marshall Cavendish Corporation
99 White Plains Road
Tarrytown, NY 10591
www.marshallcavendish.com

Library of Congress Cataloging-in-Publication Data

Dolan, Edward F., 1924-
The Pony Express / by Edward F. Dolan.
    v. cm. — (Kaleidoscope)
Includes bibliographical references and index.
Contents: Two riders, two ponies—Communications in America—Launching the Express—The Express riders—The Paiute War —The last days.
    ISBN 0-7614-1458-4
1. Pony express—History—Juvenile literature. 2. Postal service—United States—History—Juvenile literature. [1. Pony express—History. 2. Postal service—History.] I. Title. II. Kaleidoscope (Tarrytown, N.Y.)
    HE6375.P65 D65 2003
    383'.143'0973—dc21
                            2002006191

Photo Research by Anne Burns Images

Cover Photo by: Corbis/Bettman

The photographs in this book are used by permission and through the courtesy of: *Corbis:* title page, 29 Bettman, 5, 6, 21 Phil Schemeister, 17 Philip Gould, 22 Dave G.Houser; *Granger Collection:* p.9, 10, 14, 26, 30, 38, 42; *St. Joseph Museum:* 13, 25, 33; *North Wind Pictures:* 18, 34, 37; *Art Resource, NY:* 41 New York Public Library

Printed in Italy
6 5 4 3 2 1

CONTENTS

The watching crowd cheered as rider Billy Hamilton vaulted into the saddle and sent his pony racing through San Francisco to the city's dock area. At sunset on Tuesday, April 3, 1860, the little horse clattered up the gangplank of the steamer *New World*.

The *New World* dropped anchor at the city of Sacramento late that night. Billy Hamilton and his pony immediately dashed east to distant St. Joseph, Missouri. Their journey marked the start of the most unusual mail service in United States history—the Pony Express.

A rider and his appaloosa mount reenact a Pony Express run through the Nevada desert. The picture was taken in the late 1980s in honor of the Pony Express runs more than a century earlier.

That same day, another rider—Johnny Fry—vaulted into the saddle at St. Joseph. He and his pony boarded a steamboat for a trip across the Missouri River and then began a dash westward to San Francisco.

After several hours, the two riders and ponies would be relieved by other riders and mounts. At no time, however, would they slow their speed. They were living up to the promise made by the Pony Express owners. It was a promise that seemed impossible to many—to deliver letters over a distance of 1,840 miles (2961 kilometers) in just ten days.

Items such as these—ranging from pistols to branding irons—were commonly seen at all Pony Express stations.

COMMUNICATIONS IN AMERICA

The eastern half of the United States had a fine system of communications—one that extended from the Atlantic Coast all the way to Missouri. It was made up of stagecoaches, river steamboats and barges, wagons, railroad trains, and telegraph lines.

Fine though the system was, the United States government needed one that connected the Far West with the East. The nation was headed towards a civil war and without a communications system that stretched from coast to coast, the U.S. could be torn apart and be unable to mend itself.

In the first half of the nineteenth century, the nation's railroads had yet to reach the West Coast, where a fast system of mail delivery was needed. The Pony Express was designed to fill that need.

10

A few months before the Civil War began, a businessman named William Russell met with Senator William Gwin from California in Washington, D.C. Russell was a partner in two shipping companies. Alexander Majors and William Waddell were also co-owners. Their companies picked up goods that were shipped by train to Missouri, where the nation's rail system ended. Then it distributed them throughout the West by wagon.

Senator Gwin and William Russell both knew that the nation might soon be ripped apart by a civil war. They realized that a faster mail service could unite the West and the Northern states, and might help keep the country intact.

Senator William Gwin of California successfully urged William Russell to launch the Pony Express.

During the meeting, the two men came up with the idea for the Pony Express. Using fast horses and expert riders, the Pony Express would serve as a link between the East and West by swiftly delivering mail between Missouri and California. Russell was in charge of establishing a system that would deliver mail once a week in both directions. He promised to have the Pony Express ready for business in just four months, hopefully well before war broke out.

This map of the Pony Express route, with its many stops, was prepared by the historical staff of the St. Joseph Museum in Missouri. Note the various western scenes that decorate the map.

LAUNCHING THE EXPRESS

Those four months were the busiest in Russell's life. He and his partners—Alexander Majors and William Waddell—decided that the Pony Express would follow the westbound path that so many pioneer families and their wagon trains had used. Starting in St. Joseph, Missouri, it would spear through Kansas, Nebraska, Colorado, Wyoming, Utah, and Nevada. It would finally come down from the Sierra Nevada Mountains and run across northern California to end at Sacramento.

The trail used by pioneer families to travel west was not always easy—especially when traveling by covered wagon.

15

Once the route was established, Russell had to set up a string of relay stations that would provide the Pony Express with replacement mounts and riders. The stations would be placed at intervals of ten to fifteen miles (sixteen to twenty-four kilometers) and would include many that his company had built years before as wagon stops. Within a few weeks, dozens of new stations were added to the route—most of them tiny cabins—for a total of 190 in all.

This replica of a Pony Express station stands on the site of the original station in Kansas.

Over four hundred horses were purchased for the stations. Four hundred men and women were then hired to supervise the stations. They were to tend the ponies, feed the off-duty riders, purchase needed supplies, and take care of all the office work. They had to have fresh mounts ready at all times so that an arriving rider could dismount, switch his letter-filled saddle bag to the new pony, remount, and gallop off—all within a couple of minutes.

A Pony Express rider gallops toward a fresh mount at a station high in the Rocky Mountains. The stations kept more than four-hundred horses in corrals.

Finally, Russell had a special pouch fashioned to carry the mail. Called a mochila, the bag had a wide strip of leather with two pouches at either end for the letters. When changing horses during his run, a rider would toss the rig across the new saddle and then hold it in place by sitting in the saddle.

The mochila was developed by a leather worker named Isreal Landis.

When his preparations were nearing their end in March 1860, Russell placed an advertisement in a number of newspapers along the Pony Express route. One that appeared in San Francisco read,

WANTED
YOUNG, SKINNY WIRY FELLOWS NOT OVER EIGHTEEN. MUST BE EXPERT RIDERS WILLING TO RISK DEATH DAILY. ORPHANS PREFERRED. WAGES $25 PER WEEK. APPLY CENTRAL OVERLAND EXPRESS.

An enlarged version of the advertisement for Pony Express riders is seen here in the Pony Express headquarters at St. Joseph, Missouri.

23

Hundreds replied. Of their number, eighty were chosen for the job, with others to follow. It was later reported that 228 men may have ridden for the Express, though the exact number has never been known because the company records were lost.

Among their number were men whose exploits won them a lasting place in Pony Express history. Perhaps the most well known Pony Express rider was William Cody. He began riding for the Express at age sixteen and went on to win international fame as Buffalo Bill Cody.

Johnny Fry, pictured here, was the rider who made the first westward run for the Pony Express.

On one of Cody's trips, he carried the mail eastward from Red Buttes in Wyoming to a station 116 miles (187 kilometers) away. On his arrival, he learned that a rider who had been speeding west had been killed by Indians a few hours earlier. Though he had just finished an exhausting run, Bill grabbed the dead rider's mochila, mounted a fresh pony, and headed west for 76 miles (122 kilometers). Then on his arrival at the Pony Express station, he delivered the mail and once more swung into a saddle and returned eastward, this time for 192 miles (309 kilometers) back to his starting point at Red Buttes.

In total, Cody rode 384 miles (618 kilometers) without once stopping to rest. It was the longest nonstop run ever recorded by a Pony Express rider.

As a teenager, William "Buffalo Bill" Cody rode for the Pony Express and made one of the most famous trips in the company's history—a nonstop dash of 384 miles (618 kilometers). He later became well known for his traveling Wild West Show.

Many of the adventures experienced by the riders and station people occurred during an Indian uprising in the spring and summer of 1860. At that time, the Paiute tribesmen of Nevada went to war against the white settlers living among them. The Paiute hoped to drive the intruders out of their land, but they themselves soon found themselves on the run from U.S. troops. The warriors vanished into the Nevada desert and then continued to fight by burning Pony Express stations and attacking riders on the trail.

White settlers were prone to Indian attacks. The Paiute, specifically, wanted to drive them off their land.

Though many riders were targets for hostile Indians, some were very lucky. One such rider was a fifteen-year-old boy named Nick Wilson. Nick was struck by an arrow during a raid on a station where he was spending the night off-duty. The arrow lodged itself in his temple. But when he was found the next morning, he was still alive. The arrow was removed, and Wilson was soon back in the saddle after a short recovery.

In this 1861 painting, a Pony Express rider keeps an eye out for Indian attacks as he dashes across the plains. Nearby, the body of a Sioux warrior lies on a ceremonial platform before his burial.

The attacks and the losses in animals and equipment caused the Pony Express to stop its weekly runs on the last day of May 1860. But Russell and his partners replaced all that the company had lost and resumed its deliveries on June 26. The Pony Express also increased its service from one to two deliveries per week.

This letter was carried by the Pony Express on a trip that started from San Francisco on July 11, 1860, and arrived at St. Joseph on July 26 (15 days). At St. Joseph, it was placed in regular mail for New York.

Pony Express July 11th 1860

paid $10

THE CENTRAL OVERLAND CALIFORNIA
& PIKES PEAK
EXPRESS COMPANY
JULII
SAN FRANCISCO.CAL.

July 11th

SA___H
1860
MO.

Mess Eugene Kelly & Co
No 164 Fulton Street
New York

PONY EXPRESS
JUL 26
ST. JOSEPH.

33

THE LAST DAYS

Though the Pony Express was up and running again, the company was doomed to fail in just a few more months. There were two reasons for the impending failure.

First, the Pony Express was constantly losing money. To make a profit, it had to charge $5 per half ounce for its letters, a cost that was too expensive for most people. Adding to the company's problems was the $75,000 that was spent to replace the animals and equipment lost in the Paiute War.

This drawing of an Express rider and horse fighting their way through a snowstorm is representative of the troubles faced by the company in its final days.

Worst of all, the Pony Express had always hoped to win a U.S. government contract for carrying the mail. The contract would have kept the company alive, but it was never awarded one by Congress. Why? Because Congress was split between the supporters of the North and South, the two sides that, beginning in 1861, would fight the Civil War. As the war loomed, the Southern supporters blocked all Northern efforts on behalf of the Pony Express. Knowing that the Express would help the opposition, they gave a mail contract to the Butterfield stagecoach line, which ran through territory that favored the South. Until the war erupted, Butterfield received $50,000 a month under the agreement.

John Butterfield, the founder of the Butterfield stagecoach line, was quoted as saying to his drivers, "Remember boys, nothing on God's earth must stop the United States mail!"

37

The second reason for the failure was the nation's first transcontinental telegraph line. During the early days of the Pony Express, two telegraph crews were working their way towards each other. They were stringing a line from Utah to California that would connect the East and West. The two lines were finally connected on October 24, 1861.

With the telegraph, messages could be sent across the country in mere seconds. It ended the need for the Pony Express. Express service was stopped immediately and became a thing of the past.

A Pony Express rider waves as he passes workers who will soon put him out of a job.

But it was a marvelous thing of the past. The Pony Express had been in service between April 1860 and late October 1861—a mere eighteen months. Its riders had made a total of 308 complete runs in that time. They had galloped over a distance of 616,000 miles (991,000 kilometers), speeding through Indian attacks and all kinds of weather and scenery—from baking deserts in the summer to frozen rivers and mountain blizzards in winter. They had delivered 34,753 letters, with one rider killed and losing just one mochila full of mail.

This map of the late 1860s shows the telegraph lines that were already built to provide a worldwide communications system and those that were to be constructed in the near future.

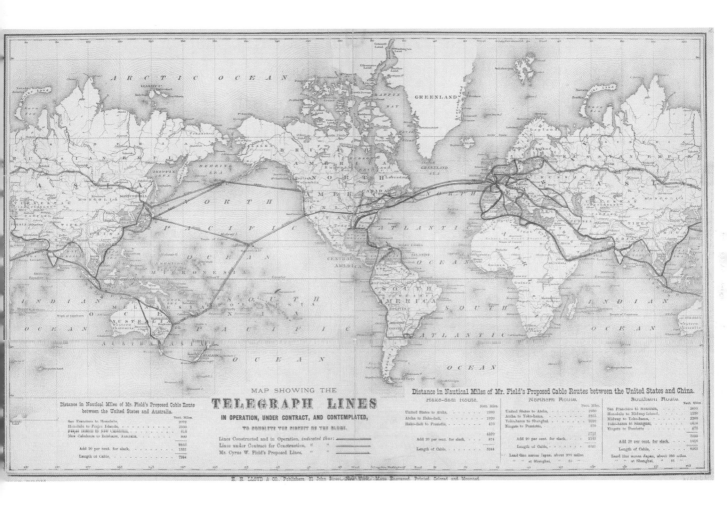

MAP SHOWING THE

TELEGRAPH LINES

IN OPERATION, UNDER CONTRACT, AND CONTEMPLATED,

TO COMPLETE THE CIRCUIT OF THE GLOBE.

Lines Constructed and in Operation, *indicated thus:* ━━━━━
Lines under Contract for Construction, " ━━━━━
Mr. Cyrus W. Field's Proposed Lines, " ━━━━━

Distances in Nautical Miles of Mr. Field's Proposed Cable Route between the United States and Australia.

	Naut. Miles.
San Francisco to Honolulu,	2092
Honolulu to Fegee Islands,	2880
Fegee Island to New Caledonia,	818
New Caledonia to Brisbane, Australia,	800
	6660
Add 20 per cent. for slack,	1333
Length of Cable,	7984

Distance in Nautical Miles of Mr. Field's Proposed Cable Routes between the United States and China.

Hako-dadi Route.

	Naut. Miles.
United States to Atcha,	1990
Atcha to Hako-dadi,	1920
Hako-dadi to Possette,	470
	4070
Add 20 per cent. for slack,	874
Length of Cable,	5244

Northern Route.

	Naut. Miles.
United States to Atcha,	1990
Atcha to Toko-hama,	2255
Yoko-hama to Shanghai,	1010
Niegata to Possette,	470
	2715
Add 20 per cent. for slack,	1145
Length of Cable,	6860
Land line across Japan, about 300 miles.	
at Shanghai,	

Southern Route.

	Naut. Miles.
San Francisco to Honolulu,	2000
Honolulu to Midway Island,	1280
Midway to Yoko-hama,	2200
Yoko-hama to Shanghai,	4610
Niegata to Possette,	470
	7060
Add 20 per cent. for slack,	1410
Length of Cable,	8463
Land line across Japan, about 250 miles.	
at Shanghai,	

H. H. LLOYD & CO., Publishers, 21 John Street, New York. Maps Engraved, Printed, Colored and Mounted.

42

The Pony Express riders and their mounts served the nation for just a few months. In the end, with the coming of the telegraph, they were of little help to the country during the Civil War. But they won lasting fame and admiration for giving the United States one of the most exciting and inspiring chapters in its history.

The Pony Express rider and horse are still deeply admired today. In this commemorative 1960 postage stamp, a rider and horse gallop across the American West.

1860 William Russell and his partners establish and equip the mail service that is to be called the Pony Express.

April 3, 1860 The Pony Express begins once-a-week mail runs between St. Joseph, Missouri, and Sacramento, California. The mail is carried by young riders on fast horses.

Spring 1860 The Paiute Indians go to war to drive white settlers out of Nevada. On being defeated by U.S. Army troops, the Indians flee into the desert and attack Pony Express stations and riders.

May 31, 1860 The Pony Express halts its mail deliveries due to the Paiute attacks.

June 26, 1860 The Pony Express resumes service and increases its deliveries to two per week.

April 12, 1861 The Civil War begins.

October 24, 1861 Work crews complete the transcontinental telegraph line, ending the need for long-distance mail service. The Pony Express stops its runs immediately.

FIND OUT MORE

BOOKS

Aylesworth, Thomas G. and Virginia L. *The West*. New York: Chelsea House, 1988.

Collins, James L. *Exploring the American West*. New York: Franklin Watts, 1989

Dicerto, Joseph J. *The Pony Express: Hoofbeats in the Wilderness*. New York: Franklin Watts, 1989.

McCall, Edith. *Mail Riders*. Chicago: Children's Press, 1980.

Memling, Carl. *The Pony Express*. New York: Parents' Magazine Press, 1962.

Stein, Conrad R. *The Story of the Pony Express*. Chicago: Children's Press, 1981.

WEBSITES

XP Pony Express Station
http://www.xphomestation.com/

AUTHOR'S BIO

Edward F. Dolan is the author of more then one hundred nonfiction books for young people and adults. He has written on medicine, science, law, history, folklore, and current social issues. Mr. Dolan is a native Californian, born in the San Francisco region and raised in Southern California. In addition to writing books, he has been a newspaper reporter and a magazine editor. He currently lives in the northern part of the state.

INDEX

Page numbers for illustrations are in boldface.